KEEP
CURIOUS
AND
CARRY A
BANANA

WISDOM FROM THE WORLD OF CURIOUS GEORGE

BY JUSTIN MARTIN & LIZA CHARLESWORTH

INSPIRED BY THE WORKS OF MARGRET & H. A. REY
WITH ILLUSTRATIONS BY H. A. REY

HOUGHTON MIFFLIN HARCOURT

BOSTON   NEW YORK

Begin each day ready to
monkey around!

Take time to smell the roses
(or eat a banana).

Clothes make the mammal.
Be bold in your
fashion choices.

A blank canvas is a brilliant opportunity.

It's a zoo out there.
So keep your
sense of humor.

Always have
an exit plan.

Be the wind beneath
your own wings.

Life is a bowl of pasta—
make sure to noodle around.

Create the world
you want to inhabit.

Stay on top of the
latest technology.
(But don't let it own you.)

Life can be a high-wire act—
the trick is keeping
your balance.

Be wildly creative!
Sometimes you need
to really turn things on
their head.

If there's an elephant
in the room, address it.
You'll sleep so much better.

Grab a great seat.
You don't want
to miss a thing.

Bring home the bacon . . .
and the donuts, too!

Multitask!
Multitask!
Multitask!

Unlock the potential
in others.

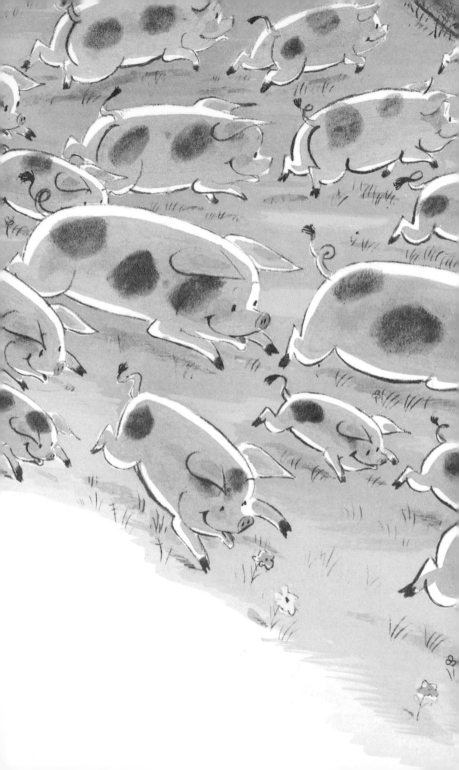

Always stay one step ahead of the crowd.

Just say yes!
Sign up for some
serious monkey
business.

Imagine the best!
Prepare to be
pleasantly surprised.

Expand
the parameters
of your job.

Make the most of a messed-up situation.

Sure, life can be a circus.

Get in the center ring!

Give
free hugs.

Read everything you
can get your paws on.

Take the road
less traveled.

There will be bumps in
the road.

The trick is to get
right back on your bike
and pop a wheelie!

Rainy day?
Who cares!

Your friends will get
you through.

Hang loose!

Don't forget
to look back.

DINOSAUR (EXTINCT)

History has much
to teach us.

Do not touch!

BABY DINOSAUR

If someone says
"Go fly a kite!"
take their advice.

If you hit a wall,
don't be discouraged.

Up and over!

Respect differences
in others.
It's much more interesting
that way!

Let them eat cake.
But save a slice
for yourself, too.

Remember,
there's more than one way
to catch a fish.

Use all your
frequent flyer miles
(some restrictions
may apply).

Don't just stand there
on the sidelines.
Get in the game!

Wisdom begins with
being puzzled.

With a little help
from your friends,
the pieces will fall
into place.

Keep curious.

Remember that every ending
is a bright new beginning.

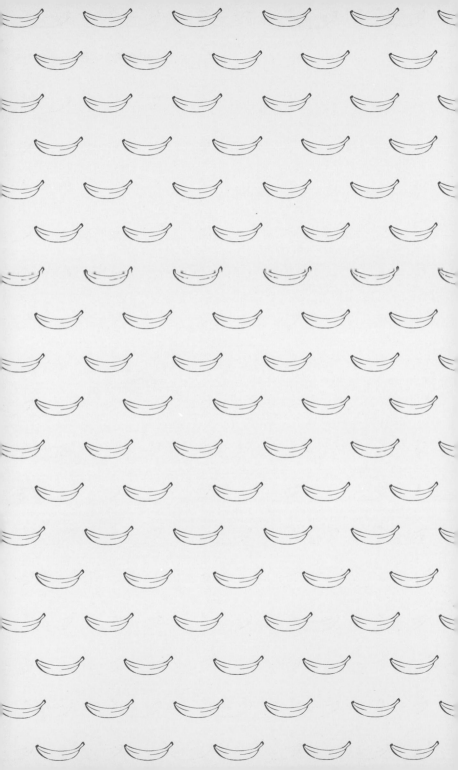